© **FRESH THOUGHTS**
BY SANDEEP RAVIDUTT SHARMA

Copyright © 2018
by Sandeep Ravidutt Sharma

All rights reserved. No part of this book may be reproduced or transmitted in any form or by any means without written permission from the author.

If you have further questions, contact on

Phone: +919969256731
Email: sandeepraviduttsharma@gmail.com

© **FRESH THOUGHTS**
BY SANDEEP RAVIDUTT SHARMA

Dedication

This book is dedicated to **Shiva Shakti** - the epitome of love. Lord Shiva is pure consciousness symbolising the masculine principle. Goddess Shakti symbolises the active feminine energy of Shiva and is synonymously identified with **Tripura Sundari, Sati** or **Parvati**. These primal principles are also called as PURUSHA representing consciousness and PRAKRITI denoting the nature. Shiva and Shakti are manifestations of the all-in-one divine consciousness. Shiva is the paternal love of God that gives us consciousness, knowledge and clarity. Shakti is the motherly love of God that showers warmth, care and ensures our protection. Shiva and Shakti *exist* within each of us as the masculine and feminine energy.
To please **Shiva Shakti** praying for the well being, love, happiness, strength, positive energy and success of my readers in their life, i hereby recite the following mantra...
"Sarva Mangala Mangalye Shive Sarvartha Sadhike Sharanye Tryambake Gauri Narayani Namostute"

© **FRESH THOUGHTS**
BY SANDEEP RAVIDUTT SHARMA

Table of Contents

Foreword IV
Fresh Thoughts................... 1

© **FRESH THOUGHTS**
BY SANDEEP RAVIDUTT SHARMA

Foreword

This book provides you with a list of **100** quotes and thoughts about LIFE, churned out by my mind with the consciousness, grace and energy of Shiva Shakti. I'm sure if you keep reading, referring and sharing these thoughts and quotes about LIFE, you may derive inspiration and develop good understanding of various perspectives and facts. To create a positive environment all around, you don't need too much of knowledge and exploration, all you need is to conceive fresh and positive thoughts that can change this world for the good.

"Gift bouquet of fresh thoughts to yourself and enjoy peace, tranquility and joyfulness."

I sincerely hope, you will find this book amazing, interesting, rejuvenating, unique and a constant source of Inspiration.

Thank You and Happy Reading.

© **FRESH THOUGHTS**
BY SANDEEP RAVIDUTT SHARMA

Photo Credits

The beautiful photograph used for the book cover is clicked by **Inger Margrethe Mo** from **Norway**.

You can visit her excellent photo gallery at

Instagram: @gotefrua1

FRESH THOUGHTS

© **FRESH THOUGHTS**
BY SANDEEP RAVIDUTT SHARMA

Fresh thoughts wake you up from dreams of yesterday and inspire to create reality of tomorrow.

© **FRESH THOUGHTS**
BY SANDEEP RAVIDUTT SHARMA

Great experience starts from self and continues with the world and beyond.

Your best is on its way. Do enough to meet it today.

Forgive others, and you can do a favour to yourself and stay lighter.

© **FRESH THOUGHTS**
BY SANDEEP RAVIDUTT SHARMA

Every generation has a responsibility to protect its heritage and value history.

Let life talk with you whether you are happy or sad.

Have patience and wait for the perfect time. Your efforts will pay you with SUCCESS.

© **FRESH THOUGHTS**
BY SANDEEP RAVIDUTT SHARMA

You may get lost in the crowd, if you don't do enough to win and succeed in life.

© **FRESH THOUGHTS**
BY SANDEEP RAVIDUTT SHARMA

Words dipped in colour create a profound effect on one's mind.

Don't misunderstand others before trying to understand their perspective.

Don't just stand at the crossroads of life, use your experience and instincts, to choose the way forward.

Critics help you to reinvent but are often listed as enemy no. 1. Thank your critics who don't allow you to deviate.

You are the best. The world is waiting for you to cheer and make everyone laugh. Greet everyone you meet with a smile and you are no more a stranger to them.

If you lose money today, you can earn it tomorrow. But if you lose respect, you may take years to build it again.

Treasure of happiness grows when you laugh.

© **FRESH THOUGHTS**
BY SANDEEP RAVIDUTT SHARMA

Competition to scale higher in life can never end. Why not think beyond the Sky to meet the Lord?

Go back in time not to count your failures but for remembering the lessons learnt.

Beauty lies in our mind.

The great match starts with a focussed approach.

Giving your best is not an option if you want to win.

Appreciate good intentions and attract noble deeds.

© **FRESH THOUGHTS**
BY SANDEEP RAVIDUTT SHARMA

Focus on your game and you can win.

Joy and Sorrow exist together, it's your mind which decides what you are experiencing and why.

What one could not achieve in a lifetime someone achieves in a day. Your level of focus decides the result.

When you win, your signature becomes an autograph.

Fragrance of the flowers can't go far unless it's involved in a relationship with the Wind.

Commit to these words, 'I'm here to resolve.'

Walk alone if you don't find the right company. Lord is always with you.

Wonderful are the ways of the Lord. You meet to part ways on one hand. On the other hand those who had lost hopes meet again.

Whenever the key of efforts meets the lock of challenges, the door of Success opens up.

Brilliant ones are those who don't wait for tomorrow to realise their dreams.

You need to ask the right questions if intend to find an innovative solution.

Take chances in life and you may win.

© **FRESH THOUGHTS**
BY SANDEEP RAVIDUTT SHARMA

Innocence never fears anyone.

© **FRESH THOUGHTS**
BY SANDEEP RAVIDUTT SHARMA

The hands of the clock meet sometimes and create an illusion of time taking a pause, but the very next moment begins its forward march.

© **FRESH THOUGHTS**
BY SANDEEP RAVIDUTT SHARMA

Mankind can thrive if nature is part of its growth plans. Go green and let life flourish.

© FRESH THOUGHTS
BY SANDEEP RAVIDUTT SHARMA

Let's create the magic of Sunshine with your beautiful mind and kind heart.

Winning attitude is ready to face challenges anytime.

The rise of the Sun fills up Positivity all around and refreshes your mind.

Avoid over commitment to stay relevant and trustworthy.

Feeling secure is a matter of the mind and not about some safety gadgets.

The magic of good listening lies in understanding things before it is explained.

Don't spend time in finding ways to impress the world. Just impress the one who looks into your mirror before you do

Fortunate ones are those who get what they want. Truly gifted ones are those who give or share what they have got.

Fresh thoughts create new ideas.

How many moments you have lived counts more than the years of your life.

The joy of living lies in the fresh thoughts created by a wonderful mind.

Colour energizes your words.

The challenges we face define the worth of our efforts.

Bright words illuminate the World.

Don't park your life when it's time to drive.

Blessings come in disguise and showers on you once satisfied.

Don't underestimate your own abilities.

Laughter makes you remember those who brought it home.

Great thoughts give birth to great things on earth.

© **FRESH THOUGHTS**
BY SANDEEP RAVIDUTT SHARMA

Experience life as it comes to you with a Smile.

Whatever you do in the name of the Lord turns into Gold. Start with good words, deeds and kindness.

In an attempt to maintain or save your reputation don't lose your character.

© **FRESH THOUGHTS**
BY SANDEEP RAVIDUTT SHARMA

Write your positive thoughts today. You never know when you would need these to inspire yourself.

Tomorrow is hard to meet as Today keeps coming before it.

Contribute towards nation building in whatever capacity you can.

Don't just look at the hungry faces and criticise the Lord. Appreciate the hands that feed the hungry inspired by the Lord.

© **FRESH THOUGHTS**
BY SANDEEP RAVIDUTT SHARMA

Everything in this Universe is changing. Be the Change in someone's life for the good.

Don't push yourself towards the Wall but on the bridge to progress connecting the mankind.

Your ability to choose is tested when life throws option at you.

Don't give up your dreams just because you failed. Try again and you can achieve.

Mankind thrives on innovation.

If you just want to reach your destination, then speed is the key. Everything blurs out in the process, and you don't see much during your journey. Don't follow this rule for the journey of your life. Don't just run but enjoy each moment of your life.

Language of LOVE doesn't need an interpreter.

Hope constantly walks ahead of you.

Declare your plan, and commitment, get involved in the execution, and success will be all yours.

Your words can create positive impact, and your good deeds can inspire.

Wonderful things happen in life when you are ready to receive them.

Let hope live even when you are facing your end.

Those who have learned from their last fall are likely to emerge victorious next time.

Don't stop if the race is on and you need to win.

If you start counting what all you have lost or gained in life, you will lose the present. Live now and forget about the calculation.

Love never dictates but persuades.

Trust defines your relationship.

To see through the darkness one has to lit the lamp.

Don't struggle for someone's attention, instead rise in life so high that you are visible to the whole world.

Thank the Lord for making you understand about Gratitude.

Those who crave to win don't expect others to work on their behalf.

© **FRESH THOUGHTS**
BY SANDEEP RAVIDUTT SHARMA

Beautiful day promises colours of joy and happiness. Let's make it amazing together.

© **FRESH THOUGHTS**
BY SANDEEP RAVIDUTT SHARMA

Wonderful are the ways of the Lord, you start your journey with a tiny step and he takes you to places far and near.

Those who welcome joy and sorrow with equal fervour are the ones who have gained mastery over their mind and three modes of nature i.e. goodness, passion and ignorance.

Today's expert was a novice of yesterday.

Wonderful are the ways of the Lord. You may lose your wealth today but your good character may inspire generations to come.

© **FRESH THOUGHTS**
BY SANDEEP RAVIDUTT SHARMA

Your timely decision can save someone's life.

The world ignores when you are not prepared and hardly focussed. World cheers for the one with a focussed mind who wins.

Colourful thoughts with a grey shade paint our existence. Live now with whatever comes your way.

Walk together on the shore and enjoy the cool breeze.

The explorer of life is fine with both happiness and sorrow.

Vibrant colours wake up your creativity.

Giving a rose is symbolic but the essence lies in your wishes behind it. You handover the beauty and fragrance of your deeper thoughts, wishes or love in the form of a ROSE.

Love is all about sharing and caring for each other.

Your thoughts bring a smile on my face.

You alone have to pay for your life journey with your actions and emotions.

You cannot buy peace of mind but can find it within.

Light the path of those who are trying to come out of darkness of ignorance through your knowledge.

www.ingramcontent.com/pod-product-compliance
Lightning Source LLC
Chambersburg PA
CBHW031439210526
45464CB00005B/2270